G000094552

from Bath *to* *the* Quantocks

Compiled by Dennis and Jan Kelsall

JARROLD
publishing

Mapping
sourced from

Ordnance
Survey®

Text: Dennis and Jan Kelsall
Photography: Dennis and Jan Kelsall
Editor: Geoffrey Sutton
Designer: Ellen Moorcraft

© Jarrold Publishing 2002

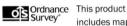 Ordnance Survey® This product includes mapping data licensed from Ordnance Survey® with the permission of the Controller of Her Majesty's Stationery Office. © Crown Copyright 2002. All rights reserved. Licence number 100017593. Pathfinder is a registered trade mark of Ordnance Survey, the national mapping agency of Great Britain.

Jarrold Publishing ISBN 0-7117-2085-1

While every care has been taken to ensure the accuracy of the route directions, the publishers cannot accept responsibility for errors or omissions, or for changes in details given. The countryside is not static: hedges and fences can be removed, field boundaries can alter, footpaths can be rerouted and changes in ownership can result in the closure or diversion of some concessionary paths. Also, paths that are easy and pleasant for walking in fine conditions may become slippery, muddy and difficult in wet weather, while stepping-stones across rivers and streams may become impassable.

If you find an inaccuracy in either the text or maps, please write or e-mail to Jarrold Publishing at one of the addresses below.

First published 2002
by Jarrold Publishing

Printed in Belgium
by Proost NV, Turnhout. 1/02

Jarrold Publishing
Pathfinder Guides, Whitefriars,
Norwich NR3 1TR
E-mail: pathfinder@jarrold.com
www.jarroldpublishing.co.uk/
pathfinders

Front cover: The bridge below Ilford manor, near Westwood
Previous page: Velvet Bottom

Contents

Keymap

SCALE 1:384 615 or 1 INCH to about 6 MILES *1CM to 3.8KM*

0   2   4   6   8   10 KILOMETRES 15

0   2   4   6   MILES 8   10

KEYMAP HEIGHTS SHOWN IN FEET

Introduction

The routes and information in this book have been devised specifically with families and children in mind. All the walks include points of interest as well as a question to provide an objective.

If you, or your children, have not walked before, choose from the shorter walks for your first outings. The purpose is not simply to get from A to B but to enjoy an exploration, which may be just a steady stroll in the countryside.

The walks are graded by length and difficulty, but few landscapes are truly flat, so even shorter walks may involve some ascent. Details are given under Route Features in the first information box for each route. But the precise nature of the ground underfoot will depend on recent weather conditions. If you do set out on a walk and discover the going is harder than you expected, or the weather has deteriorated, do not be afraid to turn back. The route will always be there another day, when you are fitter or the children are more experienced or the weather is better.

Bear in mind that the countryside also changes. Landmarks may disappear, gates may become stiles, rights of way may be altered. However, with the aid of this book and its maps you should be able enjoy many interesting family walks in the countryside.

Somerset – from Bath to the Quantocks

From the breezy heights of Ham Hill to the vast levels and moors that lie barely above the sea, Somerset's landscapes are as varied and engagingly beautiful as any in the country, marking a division between the gentle, rolling countryside that epitomises England and something hinting of a more rugged and independent nature. Though sandwiched between the two, it has much that is uniquely its own, both expressed in its contours that have been fashioned and clothed by nature and the changes wrought by man since his first settlement. This selection of walks explores a part of that land, from Bath to the Quantocks, seeking out its different moods and introducing fascinating places that reflect its history and loveliness.

In following them, you will discover some of the best places to enjoy Somerset's natural scenery and wildlife habitats.

Monkton Farleigh

Somerset's Uplands

In the east lies a band of oolitic limestone, part of the great swathe that sweeps across England from the Humber to Lyme Bay. Here, as elsewhere, it is valued as a building stone, and its subtle changes and textures are mirrored in the differing characters of the towns and villages that dot its undulating valleys and hilltops. In contrast is the landscape of the Mendip Hills, one of two Areas of Outstanding National Beauty (AONBs) in the county. Also of limestone, but of the carboniferous type, its complexion is hard, grey and bare, fractured by deep gorges and dry valleys that are honeycombed with spectacular caves such as those at Cheddar and Wookey. To the west lie the Quantock Hills, the country's first AONB. Founded on sandstones and shales, they are clad in a wonderful mantle of oaken woodland and heath. Their secluded combes and airy hill-tops were a source of inspiration to the Romantic poets Coleridge and Wordsworth and, still relatively untouched, they are little short of a walkers' paradise.

The Levels and Coast

Yet another landscape type is found in the huge expanse of flatness that runs north from the Quantocks. Once a great fenland, the coastal levels and lower-lying peat moors that spread inland behind them have been reclaimed for farming over the centuries by the construction of a vast network of drainage ditches, called rhynes. Now a wetland site of considerable importance, it sustains a rich variety of animal and plant life. Somerset's coast is also worth exploring. Although lacking dramatic cliffs, it supports several important habitats and, with an outlook to the Welsh coast, almost any vantage guarantees a fine view on a clear day.

Perhaps surprisingly, the coast holds the record for the second-greatest tidal range in the world, varying by as much as 47ft (14m) between high and low water.

An Ancient Land

Relics of our prehistoric ancestors speckle the landscape, particularly on isolated hilltops and throughout the Mendips and the Quantocks. Several burial mounds from the Stone and Bronze Ages and hillforts and settlements from the Iron Age are featured, each spectacular in its own way. Around Priddy, you will almost lose count of the burial monuments passed. Dowsborough Hillfort commands one of the finest strategic views in the county. We follow in the footsteps of the Romans, from the Mendip lead mines to the top of Ham Hill, where they conquered one of Europe's largest hillforts and began stone quarries that are still worked today.

After the Romans

Somerset lay at the heart of Anglo-Saxon Wessex, and it was at Athelney, on the marshes below Stoke St Gregory, that Alfred the Great is held to have burnt the cakes. Alfred was a Christian king, and many of the village churches can trace some link to the Saxon era. King Ine founded

A barge on the Somerset Coal Canal

Muchelney's first abbey in the 8th century and the later location of a Cluniac priory at Montacute might have been influenced by its proximity to the sacred Saxon site of St Michael's Hill.

Man's Legacy

The church is often the oldest building in a community and many aspects of the place's history can be gleaned from its stones and monuments which offer a tapestry of changing architectural style. Those visited have some wonderful examples of English craftsmanship, with carvings in both wood and stone, paintings and stained glass. The walks pass other buildings too, allowing you to contrast the ruins of a medieval castle with those of a much earlier Norman fortification. Architecture from later periods is also represented, such as the Priest's House at Muchelney, and a splendid Elizabethan mansion at Montacute. At Iford there is an opportunity to visit a wonderful garden laid out at the beginning of the 20th century by the architect Harold Peto. At Nine Springs we explore a park of a different type, a natural valley tamed by a Victorian landscaper.

Not to be overlooked is Somerset's commercial past. Bristol was once a major port but centuries before that, the Romans exported lead from the Mendips across their empire. During the medieval period, a whole host of industries thrived. Many were based on the wool and cloth, but tanning and leather, paper, quarrying and coal and metal ore mining were amongst those also important in creating wealth. At Wookey you will find a working paper mill, and hidden in a valley outside Mells are the remains of a once-busy iron foundry. Walk from Stoke St Gregory and you can learn about one of Somerset's oldest trades, willow weaving, still carried out using traditional materials and methods. The routes also touch on the transport revolution that had a large part to play in boosting Somerset's economy during the industrialisation of Britain. The Kennet and Avon Canal was built to link Bristol and London and its two aqueducts, at Avoncliff and by Monkton Combe, carrying it above the Avon gorge, were spectacular achievements of their time. The railways followed about 100 years later, criss-crossing the county with their maze of tracks. Much of the network was abandoned during the middle of the 20th century, a victim to the convenience of road transport. But the courses of some are now designated footpaths, and like that across the marshes at Langport, support a rich variety of plants.

The whole area is well covered by an extensive web of quiet tracks and paths, and several long-distance trails have been created, such as the riverside Parrett Trail, and the Greenway, which links the villages and hamlets around the foot of the Quantocks. Yet, with so much diversity and a wealth of interesting places, it can be difficult to decide just where to go. But this collection guides you to some of the most rewarding places, whetting your appetite to discover more of this county.

1 *Cadbury Camp*

START Tickenham Court

DISTANCE 2¾ miles (4.4km)

APPROXIMATE TIME 1½ hours

PARKING Roadside parking by Tickenham church

ROUTE FEATURES Moderate climb, field paths may be muddy after rain

Dotted about the Somerset moors like islands, which indeed many of them once were, are numerous hills. Dry havens offering superb vantages over the surrounding countryside, they attracted the earliest inhabitants of the area, and many bear traces of ancient settlement. Few, however, are as impressive as Cadbury Camp, the object of this interesting walk, which climbs a high ridge overlooking Nailsea.

The church at Tickenham

With the church on your right, follow church Lane onto the Causeway, leaving just after the bend through a gate on the right onto Tickenham Moor. Walk away beside a broken boundary, shortly following it right to a gate. Continue to a humped bridge and another gate, beyond which, bear left to join and follow the field edge. Right of the corner, a bridge and stile lead to a small paddock. Cross to a stile beneath a horse chestnut tree opposite; from here an enclosed path rises to Clevedon Road.

PUBLIC TRANSPORT Bus service from Bristol and Clevedon along the B3130 (alternative start)

REFRESHMENTS Pub nearby on the B3130

ORDNANCE SURVEY MAPS Explorer 154 (Bristol West & Portishead) and Landranger 172 (Bristol & Bath)

A Turn left, crossing to a waymarked stile between two houses 50 yds (46m) along. A path leads to the hill behind. Keep going beside a high fence, but, emerging from scrub, bear left to a path that undulates through Baye's Wood. Remain with the main trail, which eventually curves right and then ascends more steeply to a stile. Continue upward through a fringe of trees by open grazing, finally leaving, over a stile at the top left corner.

? *How was the way into Cadbury Hillfort defended?*

B Turn right onto a broad track, Cadbury Camp Lane West, which climbs over the hill. On a clear day, there are fine views both across the Bristol Channel and inland over the Levels, and just ahead, to the right, are the western ramparts of

Although dated as a late **Iron Age camp**, the find of a bronze spearhead suggests an even earlier occupation. Cadbury's earthen banks and complex entrance are an impressive sight, but imagine them much higher and crowned by a stake fence, a formidable obstacle to any would-be attacker already wearied by climbing the hill. However, such defences were little deterrent to the Romans, and although nothing suggests that they took the place by force, the discovery of an altar stone to the god Mars and a double-ditched, square enclosure, probably a Roman marching-camp, indicate they too valued its strategic position.

Cadbury hillfort. Beyond the summit, the track descends into trees, shortly passing the entrance to the camp **C**.

Return to the track at the entrance to the camp and continue down. Shortly, look for a bridleway

through a gate on the right, just before a house. Drop below the hill and go past a golf course. Carry on over a stile and around Folly Farm to its entrance. Ignore a drive to the golf course and walk down to the main road **D**. Washing Pound Lane opposite leads you back to the church. ●

The dedication to St Quiricus and St Julietta, two Roman martyrs, suggests an early foundation to the church, and traces of Saxon construction can be found in its stonework. More evidence of early settlement lies just to the west, where a low ring work was the site of a 12th-century castle. It was built during the first English civil war, when Stephen and Matilda fought for the throne after the death of Henry I. The present Tickenham Court, now a farm, is centred around a great hall, which was built in the 14th century and extended some 200 years later.

The earthen ramparts of Cadbury Camp

Brean Down

A stiff climb at the beginning is quickly rewarded by magnificent views in every direction. The walk continues with an easy, undulating stroll, which eventually drops to an impressive fort at the tip of the promontory. Recently restored, it provides a fascinating glimpse to a time when Britain was being fortified against an expected invasion by Napoleon III.

START Brean Bird Garden
DISTANCE 3 miles (4.8km)
APPROXIMATE TIME 2 hours
PARKING Car park near Bird Garden
ROUTE FEATURES Steep climb at start of walk, unguarded cliff edges

2

The southern flank of Brean Down, jutting out into the Bristol Channel, runs for over a mile (1.6km) in an unbroken line of rounded cliffs, almost 200ft (61m) high. The way up is by a staircase, which you will find behind the Bird Garden. Pause for a well-earned rest at the top, beside the ruins of a wartime observation point **A**.

The fort on Brean Down was blown up in 1900, but not by any invading army, what happened?

All the hard work is now over and the route to the first summit lies left, along a gently climbing grassy path. At just under 260ft (97m)

Although bounded by cliffs and steep slopes, the top of **Brean Down** is relatively level and was large enough to support a prehistoric settlement. Cleared of its trees, the land was suitable for both grazing and agriculture, and the cliffs and surrounding sea provided a natural defence against the opportunist raids of neighbouring clans. The low earthworks around the summit triangulation pillar trace boundaries between ancient fields.

PUBLIC TRANSPORT Bus service from Bridgwater
REFRESHMENTS Café at Bird Garden
PUBLIC TOILETS Near car park
PLAY AREA In Jubilee Park, by the car park
ORDNANCE SURVEY MAPS Explorer 153 (Weston-super-Mare & Bleadon Hill) and Landranger 182 (Weston-super-Mare)

above the sea, the top provides stunning views along the Channel as well as inland across the Levels. It is easy to imagine this as the island it once was, before the marshes were finally drained to provide valuable pasture on which cattle could be grazed.

Ahead, the way falls before rising again to the second summit, which, at an altitude of almost 320ft (97m), is the highest point of the ridge. As you continue, there is a wonderful view across the Channel, straight to Steep Holm, which lies about 3½ miles (5.6 km) out to sea. The other island, further away to the right is Flat Holm and has a lighthouse on its rocky point. The path follows the length of the ridge down,

ultimately dropping right to the fort at its western end.

> The **fort** was one of many built along the country's coasts during the 1870s to resist an expected invasion by the French. Although rumours abounded that secret agents, and even Napoleon himself, landed by night at secluded coves along the south coast, the assault never came. The defences were re-armed during the two World Wars and the remnants of military occupation from both centuries now lie side by side.

28

Sprat Beach

Howe Rock

Brean Down Fort
(disused)

Cairns

The view across the bay to Weston-super-Mare

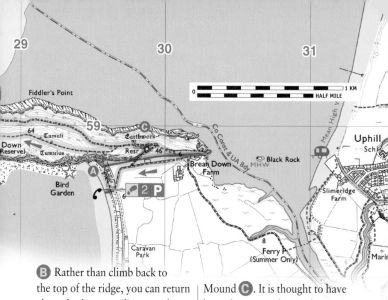

B Rather than climb back to the top of the ridge, you can return along the former military road, a track contouring the less-steep northern flank of the outcrop. Towards the far end, just after the track crests, look to the right for an earthwork, known as Pillow Mound **C**. It is thought to have been thrown up during the medieval period as a rabbit warren. Shortly beyond there, the track turns around the eastern end of the Down before dropping back to the Bird Garden.

Brean Down overlooking miles of sandy beach

Rock of Ages ● spectacular views ● woodland and heath ● nature reserve

3 *Around Burrington Combe*

Overlooked by Black Down, the highest point of the Mendip Hills, is Burrington Combe, a dark and narrow chasm that is now a dry valley. Although the road through is busy and offers little pleasure to the walker, this route around its surrounding hills offers glimpses into the gorge's wooded depths and delightful views across the countryside.

START Foot of Burrington Combe

DISTANCE 3 miles (4.8km)

APPROXIMATE TIME 2 hours

PARKING Roadside car park at foot of Burrington Combe

ROUTE FEATURES Moderate climb, woodland paths may be muddy

From the car park, walk down past the Burrington Inn and garden centre, then turn right into a lane, Ham Link. Follow it up to a junction by a triangular green and bear right. Continue climbing to the top of the hill and then go right on to a marked bridleway.

A Climb through woodland on a gradually rising path, which ultimately winds up to meet a broad track. Walk left and continue the ascent, now on more open heath. Follow the main path up a last rise, which eases towards the top. There is then a fine view back across the countryside to the coast.

Over the crest, the path now falls gently past a track from the left. Carry on ahead, the way subsequently joined by a footpath from the right. It leads across the nature reserve to Long Rock, the high point on the

Although smaller and, perhaps, less-obviously dramatic than its near neighbour, Cheddar Gorge, **Burrington Combe** was formed by a similar process. Its cliff-like sides, however, are almost obscured by trees, which manage to find a foothold in the crevices of the rock.

REFRESHMENTS Café and pub at foot of Burrington Combe

PUBLIC TOILETS Adjacent to car park at start of walk

ORDNANCE SURVEY MAPS Explorer 141 (Cheddar Gorge & Mendip Hills West) and Landranger 182 (Weston-super-Mare)

16 WALK 3 *Around Burrington Combe*

common, and the splendid views from there make it a worthy detour. However, the onward route lies ahead, shortly dropping through a belt of trees to emerge on to the road at the top of the combe.

A refuge from the storm inspired by the famous hymn

B Turn right and walk up the road for about 200 yds (183m) to a

? *Why is the huge rocky wall, which towers above the road opposite the car park, called 'Rock of Ages'?*

bridleway on the right. A gently rising track leads to an open heath beneath Beacon Batch. At a crossing **C**, turn right and then fork right. At a waymark, just further on, the route divides to

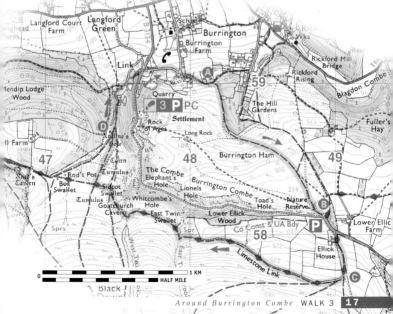

The view north from the top of Burrington Ham

run either as a footpath through the perimeter of the trees or a wider bridlepath at the edge of the moor.

The way now undulates gently along the fringe of open heath and occasionally offers fine views across Burrington Combe through breaks in the trees. Further on, the route dips to cross the head of a wooded gully, East Twin Swallet, emerging only to dip again across a second gully shortly after.

Eventually, a track joins from the left. Keep ahead to a waymarked crossing, a little further on. Turn right and follow it down, shortly reaching a stone track opposite a wooden cabin.

In spring and early summer, the limestone commons support a rich variety of flowers such as **wild thyme**, **marjoram** and **rock rose**, which in turn encourage numerous insects. Keep your eyes open for butterflies such as the common blue and meadow brown, and the strikingly patterned burnet moth. There are lots of grasshoppers here too. Walk quietly through the woods and you just might catch a glimpse of a roe deer.

D Go right again, the track descending past occasional cottages and later becoming metalled. Now take a path off to the right, signed 'RUPP' (road used as public footpath). After a short drop, it ends beside a cottage. Walk out to the road, where the Burrington Inn then lies just to the right. ●

● Dramatic gorge ● views ● spectacular caves ● paper mill

Wookey and Ebbor Gorge

START Wookey
DISTANCE 2 miles
APPROXIMATE TIME 1½ hours
PARKING Roadside parking in village (car park for visitors to Wookey Hole only)
ROUTE FEATURES Steep climb, rocks slippery when wet, country lanes without footpaths

Although perhaps best known for its splendid caves, which burrow into the limestone of the Mendip Hills behind the village, Wookey has some equally magnificent scenery above the ground. This walk goes in search of that, in Ebbor Gorge. It lies just to the north-west, a deep, narrow, wooded ravine, through which an impressive path climbs to the hillside above.

🥾 Walk out of the village past Wookey Hole, bearing right at a junction towards Easton and Cheddar. Some 250 yds (229m) along, immediately after the last cottage on the right, turn beside it through a gate, signed 'Priddy and West Mendip Way'

Ⓐ Bear left along the foot of a wooded hillside field and soon climb over a stile into a wood at the bottom of Ebbor Gorge. Ignore a stepped path off to the right but, at a fork just beyond it, go right, signed 'Gorge'.

A footpath rising to the narrow gorge

PUBLIC TRANSPORT Bus service from Wells
REFRESHMENTS Pubs in village, café at Wookey Hole Visitor Centre
PUBLIC TOILETS At Wookey Hole Visitor Centre
ORDNANCE SURVEY MAPS Explorer 141 (Cheddar Gorge & Mendip Hills West) and Landranger 182 (Weston-super-Mare)

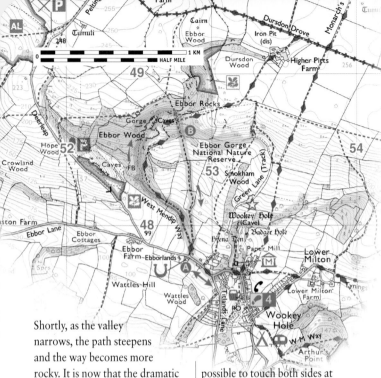

Shortly, as the valley narrows, the path steepens and the way becomes more rocky. It is now that the dramatic nature of the gorge asserts itself, with high cliffs rising sheer on both sides. At one point it is just about possible to touch both sides at once. Little legs may find the path a bit of a scramble, but there is nothing difficult. However, do go carefully, particularly if it is wet, for the smooth limestone underfoot can be slippery. Near the top of the climb, is a rocky platform to the left above the path, from which there is a spectacular view down the gorge.

Ebbor Gorge is one of several deep and narrow ravines that cleave the steep, southern escarpment of the Mendip plateau. The river torrent that gouged it from the hard rock has long since disappeared, leaving dry the rocky river bed and steps, over which waterfalls once cascaded. Sheltered from the weather and largely untouched by man's activity, a lush woodland habitat has developed in which a rich variety of both plant and animal life thrives.

> ? *Where in Wookey will you find an elephant, a ghost and a witch's turkey?*

Wookey Hole (tel. 01749 672243) is a series of chambers dissolved from the rock and containing countless fascinating formations. In places, the River Axe runs beneath your feet, its deceptively placid waters flowing at the rate of 11m gallons (50m litres) a day. Much of Wookey's spectacular cave system is still flooded by the river, but divers have penetrated some of the higher chambers. Their discoveries, together with archaeological finds, are displayed in the cave museum.

Suddenly, the valley opens out and the climb eases, the route taking you, once again, into thick woodland. At a bend, go right, following a car park sign. Ascend a bank to a crossing of paths, where the car park is then signed right. However, instead, now walk ahead on a fainter path, which drops through the trees to emerge over a stile at the top of an open field **B**.

As you descend the hillside beyond, there is a wonderful view across Wookey to Wells. Through a gap in the bottom hedge, carry on down the subsequent fields. Finally, at the foot of the hill, you meet your outward course. Return to the lane **A** and turn left for the short walk back to the village. ●

Wookey's paper mill is the oldest of its kind still working in the country, producing high-quality paper from cotton fibre by a process unchanged in centuries. Papermaking began here in 1610, exploiting both the power and purity of the River Axe.

Fields overlooking Wookey and Wells

● Coastal views ● medieval churches ● beach

5 Kilve and East Quantoxhead

Barely 5 miles (8km) wide but running for 14 miles (22.5km) in a gentle curve across Somerset, the Quantock Hills are everywhere full of charm and character. Here at their northern extremity, where they meet the Bristol Channel, the Quantocks present a rounded shoulder of soft, undulating hills to the sea, and this walk highlights just one more aspect of their individuality.

START Kilve Pill
DISTANCE 3 miles (4.8km)
APPROXIMATE TIME 1½ hours
PARKING Coastal pay-and-display car park
ROUTE FEATURES Field paths may be muddy after rain, quiet lanes without footpaths

Go back along the track by which you arrived at the car park. Beyond the ruined chantry and adjacent tearooms is Kilve church. There, turn in beneath the lichgate at a sign to East Quantoxhead **Ⓐ**.

Leave the churchyard through a gate just past the porch and follow a track away beside the right-hand edge of a field. It continues over a stream,

The Church of **St Mary the Virgin** at Kilve Pill was founded around the 13th century and, like the nearby chantry, is said to have been used by smugglers, who landed cargoes on this lonely coast under cover of darkness. On one occasion, suspicious excise men apparently set fire to the chantry after being refused admission to search it for contraband.

passing through a field gate and on to the bottom point of East Wood. Carry on below the edge of the trees, eventually leaving through a gate in the far corner of the field. Keep straight on along a track, which leads up to a junction by a lively duck pond at East Quantoxhead. Turn right and then left into a field, used as a car park, and bear right, crossing it towards the church **Ⓑ**.

PUBLIC TRANSPORT Bus service from Bridgwater to nearby Kilve village
REFRESHMENTS Tearoom, picnic area and possibly ice-cream van at Kilve Pill
PUBLIC TOILETS Adjacent to Kilve Pill car park
ORDNANCE SURVEY MAPS Explorer 140 (Quantock Hills & Bridgwater) and Landranger 181 (Minehead & Brendon Hills)

At the heart of **East Quantoxhead** lies the **Court House**. A medieval building, it has been remodelled several times by the Luttrells, who have held the manor from the beginning of the 13th century. The adjacent church, also dedicated to St Mary the Virgin, was built in the 13th century and contains many interesting features. Look for the carvings on the pews and the unusual opening in the side of the porch, a 'coffin squint', which allowed the waiting priest to watch for the approach of a funeral.

With your back to the churchyard entrance, walk down the field, bearing right to a gate at the bottom. Continue in the same direction across the subsequent field, to leave by another gate at the far corner. Turn right along the lane, but at a left-hand bend go ahead along an

? *Where can you find a dove of peace and a unicorn at East Quantoxhead?*

ascending, hedged track. When you reach a junction at the crest of the hill **C** turn right on to a permissive path along the field edges to the coast.

Low cliffs of finely striated, soft shales fall below the coastal fields, and a path over a stile on the right takes you along their top. Undulating gently downwards, keep going along the perimeter of successive fields until you are

Kilve and East Quantoxhead WALK 5 **23**

The path to the beach at Kilve

Oil lies beneath your feet at Kilve, entrapped in the shales that form the cliffs and run below the sea. The strange building by the car park was built in the 1920s and is a retort in which the shale was roasted to release the oil compounds. However, the industry was short-lived, for the cost of production proved too great.

along the cliff path to Kilve Pill. There, you will find a grassy picnic area and you can again reach the beach. A path on the right then returns to the car park. ●

Inside the church at East Quantoxhead

forced inland beside a narrow inlet **D**. Walk up past a ruined lime kiln, half-hidden by encroaching vegetation, and then double back around it, joining a track to return to the cliffs.

At this point, steps lead down to the shore, where a spring gushes from the cliffs – and you might discover a fossil in the crumbling rock. However, the route continues

Will's Neck and the Triscombe Stone

START Blue Ball Inn, Triscombe

DISTANCE 3¼ miles (5.2km)

APPROXIMATE TIME 2 hours

PARKING Car park opposite Blue Ball Inn (additional parking higher up opposite Triscombe Quarry)

ROUTE FEATURES Steep climb

6

Although lower than many hill areas, the Quantocks are defined by close-packed contours, denoting steep-flanking slopes. Obvious too are narrow valleys, splitting each side, which sometimes rise almost to meet at the middle. This walk takes an oblique line to Will's Neck, the highest point on the range, before returning down one of its finest combes.

Follow the lane up past the Blue Ball Inn, going ahead at a junction just beyond it, towards Triscombe Quarry. After some 350 yds (320m), look for a waymarked track on the right that doubles back above the lane. An easy walk through the trees then contours the hillside above the pub, eventually to join a lane.

Ⓐ Immediately branch left on to a

> **?** What are the huge trees that form an impressive avenue by the Triscombe Stone?

gently rising track, the Quantock Greenway. Keep right where it later forks, and follow it on through the woods until you ultimately drop to a junction Ⓑ. To the left, a bridleway ascends the steep flank of Bagborough Hill. Keep climbing at a crossing track part-way up. Eventually the trees thin and the gradient eases, and the track along the top of the ridge is not far ahead. Although there is still height to gain, the hard work is over, and it is now an enjoyable walk to the summit cairn of Will's Neck, which lies less than ½ mile (800m) to the left.

REFRESHMENTS Blue Ball Inn

ORDNANCE SURVEY MAPS Explorer 140 (Quantock Hills & Bridgwater) and Landrangers 182 (Weston-super-Mare) and 193 (Taunton & Lyme Regis)

Beech trees by the Triscombe Stone

C Beyond the triangulation pillar, where there is a superb view along the western valley, bear right on to a path that drops fairly steeply

The summit survey point stands over a Bronze Age monument known as **Will's Neck Barrow**. An earth mound concealing a stone-built chamber, it is around 5,000 years old and was built as a tomb. It is one of some thirty such funerary monuments known along the Quantocks ridge, an enigmatic link with the ancient people who once settled this land.

The ancient Trisombe Stone – the subject of strange tales

The low boulder by the junction is the **Triscombe Stone**, the name deriving from 'trist' – a meeting-place. Its origins are lost in time, but some describe it as an ancient wishing stone. However, others warn of a more sinister purpose, saying that the Devil musters his spectral Yeth hounds and horsemen around it before embarking upon a frantic hunt across the moors. To see or even hear the hounds means certain death.

from the ridge. Keep going where it eventually levels and then join a track to the left, which leads to a junction of tracks near a car park.

Continue ahead past the junction along the Drove, which is lined by magnificent, wind-swept trees. A little way beyond a gate, at a dip, turn through a waymarked gate on the left **D** and walk away, dropping easily downhill along a grassy path into the deepening fold of Triscombe Combe. Lower down a more prominent track develops. Later, ignore a footpath branching through a gate on the right and keep going, shortly leaving the open hillside through a gate. Stay with the track past a farm and then, when you reach a lane at the bottom, turn left back to the Blue Ball Inn. ●

7 *The willow beds around Stoke St Gregory*

START	Parish church at Stoke St Gregory
DISTANCE	2¾ miles (4.4km)
APPROXIMATE TIME	1½ hours
PARKING	Roadside parking by church
ROUTE FEATURES	Moderate climb, field paths may be muddy, quiet lanes without footpaths

An important industry of the communities fringing the Somerset moors was weaving, using willow rods cultivated in beds on the marshy ground. This short walk passes two places where the craft is still practised, and a museum gives a fascinating insight into the process from planting to finished basket, as well as illustrating the area's natural history.

🖊 From the church, walk to a junction opposite the Royal Oak and go right. Turn left into Church Close and then right up a short cul-de-sac. You will find a footpath between the houses at its very end. Over a stile, cross a field along its right-hand hedge to emerge on to a lane.

Ⓐ Turn left, but at a thatched cottage opposite a junction, leave over a stile on the right. Walk away, continuing at the edge of a second field and on over a couple of stiles into a larger field. Now bear left, pass through a gate by a power-line post and maintain your direction to another gate, lying towards the further end of the left-hand hedge. Cross to the far corner of the next field and walk out to a track. Go past cottages to English Hurdle.

> Above the doorway of **St Gregory's Church** is a 15th-century statue of the saint carrying his emblems, a dove, book and pen. Elected pope in 590, he sent the missionary Augustine to England, and his influence on the ecclesiastical music of his day is remembered in the 'Gregorian' chants.

PUBLIC TRANSPORT Bus service from Taunton
REFRESHMENTS Royal Oak at Stoke St Gregory, tearoom at Willows and Wetlands Visitor Centre
PUBLIC TOILETS Willows and Wetlands Visitor Centre
ORDNANCE SURVEY MAPS Explorer 128 (Taunton & Blackdown Hills), Landranger 193 (Taunton & Lyme Regis)

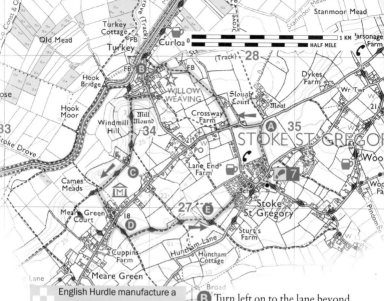

English Hurdle manufacture a range of products from willows grown on the moors. There are other craft workshops to look at too, a pottery shop and the studio of Serena de la Hey. She was commissioned to create the gigantic Willow Man sculpture, which stands beside the motorway near Bridgwater.

B Turn left on to the lane beyond, but after 200 yds (183m), cross a stile on the right. Follow the bottom field edge to another stile and then climb the hill by the left-hand hedge. Proceed through a gate at the top, continuing across the fields until you emerge beside a small waste-water treatment plant.

C Walk in front of the plant's gated entrance and then turn right, dropping through the hedge over a stile to the field beyond. Carry on beside the hedge on the

A willow teapot at the Willows and Wetlands Centre

WILLOWS & WETLANDS VISITOR CENTRE

left across successive fields until you reach a crossing track. There, go left to reach the Willows and Wetlands Visitor Centre **D**.

Just along the lane, to the right of the entrance, take a waymarked

Look for the stocks in St Gregory's churchyard. How many people can they accommodate?

track on the left, which leads into a field. Walk ahead but, as you pass into the subsequent field, turn left

A museum, video and guided tours at the Willows and Wetlands Visitor Centre describe the different stages of willow production. Displays and exhibits also tell you something of how the area has evolved over the centuries. They explain how man created the landscape we see today and indicate some of the flowers and wildlife to look for in the different habitats.

alongside the hedge. Where the boundary later moves away, bear right, crossing to a stile in a gap in the hedge ahead by overhead power-cables **E**. Over a bridge, follow the perimeter right around an indented corner of the field. Ignore a second bridge and continue walking to the corner of the hedge. There, turn right and walk along the long edge of the field.

Keep going over a stile through a paddock, beyond which you emerge between houses on to a street. The path carries on ahead at the edge of a central green and beside a school to end at the main lane through Stoke St Gregory. Turn right and then left through the village to return to the Royal Oak. ●

A thatched roof under repair

Nine Springs

Just minutes' walk from Yeovil town centre, a hill rises above the town, cleaved by a narrow valley into which streams burst from the rock, the 'nine springs'. This walk explores the paths that wind through the trees past cascades and pools in a silvan dell. The final stage follows an Easy Access Path beside the lower lakes.

START Goldenstones Leisure Centre
DISTANCE 2 miles (3.2km)
APPROXIMATE TIME 1½ hours
PARKING Pay-and-display car park at Goldenstones
ROUTE FEATURES Woodland paths may be muddy, moderate climb at start of walk

A path from the car park runs to the right behind Goldenstones. Just beyond the leisure centre, turn left beside the Memorial Garden and then leave the tarmac path to continue up the hillside by the fence. Carry on up steps into the woodland above and walk to the right on to a crossing path above the garden. The way then undulates easily upwards through the trees, later rising to more open ground at the top of the bank.

There you will find a lateral path, Beech Walk.

A Turn left and, with the climb now over, you can enjoy a pleasant

? What does the mosaic, set into the ground beneath the source spring, depict?

The country park has become a rich habitat for many species. There are badger setts amongst the trees, but unless you wait quietly after sunset you are unlikely to see their occupants. A more probable bet is a grey squirrel, scurrying amongst the undergrowth in search of food or scampering with carefree ease up the tree trunks. One of the most impressive trees in the woods is the sweet chestnut, introduced by the Romans and grown for the delicious nuts it produces in autumn.

PUBLIC TRANSPORT National bus and train services to Yeovil
REFRESHMENTS Café at leisure centre and picnic tables in park
PUBLIC TOILETS At leisure centre
ORDNANCE SURVEY MAPS Explorer 129 (Yeovil & Sherborne) and Landranger 183 (Yeovil & Frome)

the second small lake known as the Grotto Pond.

Water bubbles from the rock in several places on your right and, around the source of one spring, a small grotto has a representation of a lotus flower at its base. Remain on the same side of the water past the next dam and beside another pool, Ford Pond. When you reach the far end of that, however, turn left across a bridge and carry on downstream above Green Pond. At the bottom of that, recross the stream and walk around the shore

A wide path follows the edge of the lower lake

saunter through the trees with occasional glimpses over the town far below. Ignore paths dropping to the left, and keep going, shortly passing through a clearing. Eventually the path bends sharply left above the head of the valley.

B There, drop down beside the source spring, which gushes spectacularly from the solid rock of the hillside. The water feeds the first of a succession of pools that line the narrow, wooded gorge. Walk down past a retaining dam to

The valley was landscaped in the 1830s as a Victorian leisure garden. **Dams** created a series of babbling waterfalls and peaceful ponds, and the banks were planted with unusual plants, discovered in exotic countries by the explorers and plant-hunters of the day. Old photographs show a picturesque thatched cottage overlooking the lake, where afternoon teas were served during the summer. Unfortunately, it has long since disappeared.

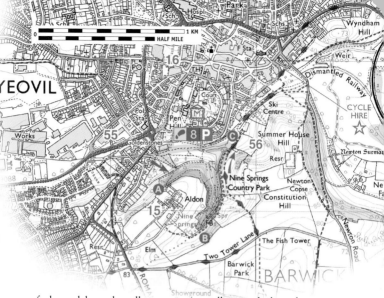

of a larger lake as the valley opens out.

C To the right, as you bear left at the foot of the lake, is a children's play area. By the water you will usually meet ducks and swans, always eager to be fed. As you leave the lake behind, turn right and then left to return through an open park to the start point at the leisure centre.

●

Swans beside the lake

9 Bathford Hill and Monkton Farleigh

START Bathford Hill

DISTANCE 4¼ miles (6.8km)

APPROXIMATE TIME 2½ hours

PARKING Car park on minor lane above Bathford

ROUTE FEATURES Woodland paths may be muddy, quiet lanes without pavements

East of Bath, the Avon squirms in a massive loop, contained within a deep, steep-sided valley below Bathford Hill. This walk winds through the lush woodland that fringes the top of the escarpment, where breaks in the trees frame grand views across the river. The return is by way of the village of Monkton Farleigh, an ancient monastic settlement.

An information board above the car park marks the start of a meandering path into the woodland. Keep ahead on the main track, passing the entrances to some of the hill's abandoned mines. Eventually, the way emerges into a clearing, a long, open terrace below the upper cliff, which overlooks the Avon valley and offers a stunning view.

Watch the skyline, ahead to your left, as you near the far end of the clearing. You will catch a glimpse of the folly, which appears briefly above the trees at the top of the cliff. A little further on, where a path rises from the right, a steep, stepped path climbs to it. The tower was

Bathford's oolitic limestone has been exploited since Roman times, extracted by mining rather than quarrying to obtain the best stone. The stone workings were abandoned in the early 20th century, and lush woodland now covers the hillside. It is rich in both plant and animal life, and the dark recesses of the derelict mines are now home to bats.

PUBLIC TRANSPORT Bus service from Bath to Monkton Farleigh (alternative start)

REFRESHMENTS King's Arms at Monkton Farleigh

CHILDREN'S PLAY AREA Along lane above car park

PUBLIC TOILETS Along lane above car park

ORDNANCE SURVEY MAPS Explorers 155 (Chippenham & Bradford-on-Avon) and 156 (Bristol & Bath), Landranger 172 (Bristol & Bath) and 173 (Swindon & Devizes)

built in the 18th century by Mr Wade-Browne, who owned the manor-house at nearby Monkton Farleigh. An internal staircase rises to a viewing platform, where windows look out to the four points of the compass. However, it is derelict inside and, until repairs have been carried out, the ascent is not safe. Return to this spot if you climb to see its base.

Ⓐ Go ahead into the trees. Ignore side paths and continue along a gently undulating path, which, after a mile (1.6km) descends to a road Ⓑ. About 100 yds (91m) to the left, leave again beside the gated entrance to a house, turning left on to a bridleway that rises from a bridge beneath the road. At the top, it bends right and, after leaving the trees, ends at a junction by Douch Farm Nursery.

Ⓒ Cross to a minor lane opposite and then, in front of some cottages, go right. At the very end of the lane, walk on through a kissing-gate into a field and turn left. Maintain your direction over successive fields and a couple of crossing tracks, making for Monkton Farleigh, which becomes visible ahead. Leave the final field

> **?** *What unusual structure is hidden in the left-hand bank of the lane, leaving Monkton Farleigh past the King's Arms?*

on to a track and continue along it below the rear of a housing estate **D**.

Beyond the houses, approaching Church Farm, watch for a field gate in the left-hand hedge. Leave the track just beyond it through an iron hand-gate into a small paddock. Cross in a diagonal towards the church, walking out to the road along a narrow path beside the graveyard. St Peter's Church dates from the 13th century and retains its original Norman zigzag decoration above the door. Inside, is a fine, carved wooden pulpit, dating from the Jacobean period.

A glimpse of the Avon Valley

The Cluniacs founded a priory in **Monkton Farleigh** in 1125, but after the Dissolution of the monasteries under Henry VIII in 1547 the estate passed to the Duke of Somerset. He built himself a manor-house on the site, and all that remains today of the priory church are ruins of the chancel wall. However, the strange-looking building in the field on the right beyond the King's Arms, known as the Monks' Conduit, covers a spring that supplied the monastery with water.

E Follow the lane beyond the church up into the village and go ahead at successive junctions to climb past the King's Arms public house.

After 300 yds (274km) **F** turn left on to a track, maintaining your direction across the field beyond. Go over a crossing track and through a small copse. As you emerge, walk left and then right to continue between open fields to a gate into the woodland ahead. At the end of a short, walled path, bear right to find a white-topped marker-post a little further on and there, turn left. Below, a stepped path drops through the trees. At the bottom, turn right and then fork right to return to the clearing below the folly **A**. Now retrace your outward steps to the car park above Bathford. ●

The Kennet and Avon Canal and Monkton Combe

START	Dundas Aqueduct Marina
DISTANCE	3½ miles (5.6km)
TIME	2 hours
PARKING	Dundas Marina and Visitor Centre car park (pay and display, locked at 21.00)
ROUTE FEATURES	Canal towpaths, woodland and field paths may be muddy, short climb

A nostalgic walk for those who remember The Titfield Thunderbolt, since Monkton Combe provided the film with its village station. Sadly, the line and halt have now gone, but the street down which Titfield's inhabitants hurried to catch the morning train is still there. On summer Sunday afternoons, you can take a trip on the canal from the marina.

Start along a track from the far end of the car park, which follows the course of a former railway line below the marina. At the far end, the track rises to join the Kennet and Avon Canal towpath. The narrow entrance to the Somerset Coal Canal lies just to the left, but your onward route lies along the towpath to the right, over the Dundas Aqueduct **Ⓐ**.

At a bridge, ¾ mile (1.2km) further on, leave the canal side to join the

The short section of canal now occupied by the marina is all that remains of the 10-mile (16km) **Somerset Coal Canal**. It operated between 1801 and 1898 and was built to service coal mines at Paulton and Radstock. The aqueduct is one of two that carry the Kennet and Avon Canal over the Avon and is named after Charles Dundas. He was chairman of the shareholders and raised £900,000 to finance the project. In its heyday, the canal carried almost 350,000 tons of cargo a year between London and Bristol.

PUBLIC TRANSPORT Bus service from Bath to Monkton Combe and Limpley Stoke and trains to Freshford near Limpley Stoke (alternative start)
REFRESHMENTS Café at marina, pubs in Limpley Stoke and Monkton Combe
CHILDREN'S PLAY AREA By route at Limpley Stoke
ORDNANCE SURVEY MAPS Explorer 155 (Bristol & Bath) and Landranger 172 (Bristol & Bath)

B3108 **B** and walk right across the River Avon and beneath a railway bridge to a junction. Go left into Limpley Stoke and, after passing the Hop Pole Inn, turn right to climb Woods Hill. Bear right at a fork part-way up and then go right again at a junction, eventually reaching the main road at the top.

> **?** *How many arches support the viaduct carrying the A36 above Midford Brook?*

emerges from the trees over a stile at the top edge of a field. Walk down, bearing left to a second stile, which takes you out on to a lane.

Turn left, but immediately fork right towards Waterhouse, continuing past its gated drive. At the lane's end, ignore another gate leading to cottages, instead drop right to follow a path above Midford Brook. Turn right over a footbridge and carry on between overgrown meadows and across a second stream **D**.

C Cross to a path directly opposite, signed 'Waterhouse'. After winding for some distance through scrub and then woodland, the way eventually

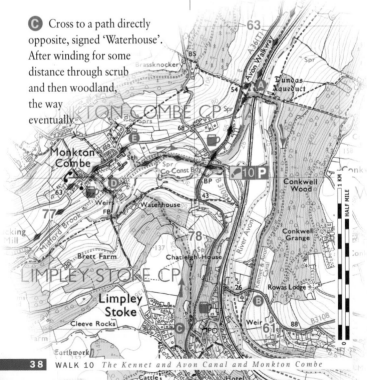

The building by the river, to the right of the bridge, was a **flax mill**, later adapted to manufacture cotton. After the market declined, it produced mattresses until the mill closed in the 1930s. The railway above was that of the Wiltshire, Somerset and Weymouth, and was built in the 1840s. It had already closed when the village was selected as the location for Titfield in the famous 1952 Ealing comedy. However, a section of track was reopened and the station refurbished for its starring role.

A path then climbs to join a lane higher up, where you cross the courses of both the former railway and the coal canal. Continue up the lane into Monkton Combe, passing a curious square building of stone on the right. It was built around 1776 as the village lock-up.

At the top, turn right through the village, passing some of its ancient buildings, which are now used by Monkton School. It was founded in 1868 by the Reverend Francis Pocock, vicar of St Michael's Church in the village, to educate the sons of missionaries.

Beyond the main school building **E**, turn into the school at a waymark. Walk down past the sports hall to a tarmac path, which continues through trees to a lane. A woodland path opposite follows it left to the school's sports field, where you can carry on along the edge of the pitches below the lane. Shortly after passing beneath an impressive viaduct carrying the A36 across the valley, leave over a stile. You will find the entrance to the car park just to the left. ●

The Kennet and Avon Canal meets the Somerset Coal Canal at Dundas Bridge

11 *Crook Peak*

Although some 625 ft (190m) above sea level, the ascent of Crook Peak is not demanding and, on a fine day, is rewarded by a wonderful view from the summit. The return through Compton Bishop, a small hamlet in a fold below, passes an ancient church, some of its structure is considered to be by the builders of Wells Cathedral.

START Cross
DISTANCE 4½ miles (7.2km)
APPROXIMATE TIME 2½ hours
PARKING Roadside parking near the White Hart Inn
ROUTE FEATURES Moderate climbs, field paths may be muddy

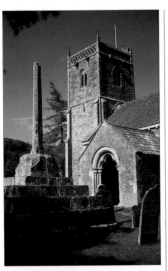

St Andrew's Church

About 200 yds (183m) west of the White Hart Inn, set back between cottages, a marked footpath on the right leads to a field behind. Walk up, crossing a stile at the top to reach the base of a quarry. Go left to a ladder-stile and then bear right over scrubby heath to a gap in the overgrown hedge opposite. Cross the next field to a stile to the right of its bottom left corner (ignore the one

> **?** Look for the church warden's chest in St Andrew's Church. How many old locks does it have and why?

PUBLIC TRANSPORT Bus service from Weston-super-Mare
REFRESHMENTS Snacks and meals at the White Hart Inn
ORDNANCE SURVEY MAPS Explorer 153 (Weston-super-Mare & Bleadon Hill) and Landranger 182 (Weston-super-Mare)

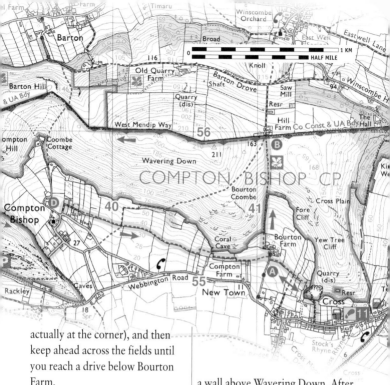

actually at the corner), and then keep ahead across the fields until you reach a drive below Bourton Farm.

Ⓐ Go right and then follow the drive left in front of the farmhouse through a gate. There, turn right and climb to the left-most gate at the top corner of the field. Continue along a meandering path through bracken and bramble up Bourton Combe. Keep on where the way levels towards Hill Farm, which lies beside a stand of massive beech and sycamore trees on the summit ridge Ⓑ.

A broad track then rises left beside a wall above Wavering Down. After dropping to a saddle, climb again over Compton Hill, the way falling beyond to another saddle and a crossing of paths. That on the left is the eventual way down, but first carry on ahead to the top of Crook Peak. The last few yards of the direct ascent present an easy scramble, but it can be avoided by a short detour around the side.

Ⓒ Retrace your steps to the saddle and go right. Ignore crossing paths, but lower down, where the way 'kisses' a parallel path, drop left on to that. The path then passes into a wood, shortly leading through a gate. Immediately beyond that, turn sharp left to double back through another gate and follow a track down into the village. At the bottom, go left towards the church.

The Saxons gave the name **Compton** to the village, with 'Bishop' added later when the manor was held by the bishops of Wells. Parts of St Andrew's Church, the south doorway and font, are 12th century. Many of the pews have a door, but those at the back and along the north aisle do not and are labelled 'free'. Refurbishment grants often carried a condition that some seats remain 'free', in days when affluent church-goers 'rented' for their private pews.

D Follow the lane around the front of the church, but instead of turning right at the next corner go ahead on a track. Go right behind a row of houses and, at the end, carry on over a stile into a field. Keep ahead across the fields, eventually bearing left to skirt a house and its garden, following the boundary to a stile. Maintain the same heading beyond, until you finally emerge over a stile on to the drive that runs below Bourton Farm **A**.

Cross directly over and continue through the fields, retracing your outward steps to the foot of the quarry. There turn right and walk down, back out to the lane. ●

A path undulates across Wavering Down

Priddy and its burial mounds

START Priddy Green
DISTANCE 4 miles (6.4km)
APPROXIMATE TIME 2 hours
PARKING Roadside parking around Priddy Green
ROUTE FEATURES Moderate climb, field paths may be muddy, quiet lanes without footpaths

The Mendips were settled by prehistoric farmers, and enigmatic traces of their presence lie scattered throughout the hills. However, nowhere are they more spectacularly concentrated than around Priddy, where numerous barrows corrugate the skyline of North Hill. To reach them, the walk passes old lead mines, whose abandoned hollows and spoil heaps are now an important wildlife habitat.

Head north up a lane beside Manor Farm, which overlooks the green. Bear off right through a barrier along a drive to the church and then turn right in front of the adjacent school. Priddy is the highest village in Somerset, with its church, St Laurence's, standing even higher. Inside, stone benches line the walls, seats for the old and sick in a time before there were pews and the congregation stood to hear the service.

Ⓐ Beyond the school, cross a stile and walk ahead to the furthest corner of the field, where it narrows to a point. Climb over a

The hurdle stack at Priddy

PUBLIC TRANSPORT Bus service from Wells
REFRESHMENTS Pubs in Priddy
ORDNANCE SURVEY MAPS Explorer 141 (Cheddar Gorge & Mendip Hills West) and Landranger 182 (Weston-super-Mare)

stile and keep going in the same direction, making for another stile, to the right of a gate on the far boundary. Climb beside a wall in the next field and, through a gate at the top, bear right. From a ladder-stile, head towards Eastwater Farm and into a caravan field. Turn right past the farm buildings and walk out to East Water Lane.

? *Keep your eyes open on the way to Priddy church to discover when the first pure water supply was installed in the village.*

B Some 50 yds (46m) along to the right, pass through a gate on the left and bear right, walking the length of the next couple of fields. A deepening gully over to the left abruptly terminates at a sinkhole,

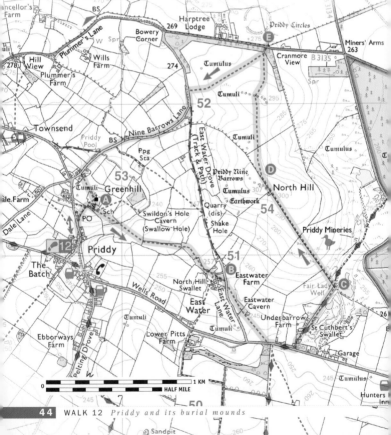

Eastwater Cavern. Continue beyond to leave the field on to a lane, Wells Road, and turn left.

After passing a couple of cottages, go left on a track to Underbarrow Farm. Where it bends, walk ahead, signed 'Priddy Pool', in front of a building and on over a stile on to a track. Cross a second stile opposite and then follow an undulating path beside the overgrown site of old lead workings. Further on, the way runs beneath trees, bringing you to a crossing of paths under a large beech tree.

Known as **Priddy Mineries**, the area was once extensively worked for its lead ore, perhaps since Roman times. Because of lead contamination, the land is now unsuitable for grazing, and nature has been left to re-colonise the old spoil heaps and pits. The site is now a nature reserve and home to many species, particularly plants, reptiles and invertebrates.

C Go left, loosely following a wall up the edge of rough ground on to North Hill. At the top, cross a stile into a meadow and continue beside the wall past Priddy Barrows.

After passing the final prominent mound **D** bear right towards a stile and continue across the next field. Two more barrows stand to the left and, in front, a whole herd of them graze the skyline. Pass between them and continue to a gate by a break in the trees at the far side of the field. Look across the road towards

Priddy Pool and the surrounding land provide a valuable nature reserve

Some of the barrows above Priddy

In the field to the left, at the top of North Hill, lie a string of Bronze Age burial mounds, known as **Priddy Nine Barrows.** Six of them are particularly prominent, forming a dramatic sequence along the horizon. None is open, so resist climbing the wall into the adjacent field.

Priddy Circles, four earthwork enclosures that stand in a line, slightly east of due north. Each is about 180 yds (165m) in diameter and defined by a low bank and shallow ditch.

E Return to the field and bear right to walk past the far end of the barrows. Leave by a gate on to Nine Barrows Lane and go left. After ½ mile (800m), just beyond a cottage on the left, turn down beside it and go through a gate into a field. Carry on towards the church, walking past it to reach the drive beyond **A**.

Retrace your outward route back to the village green, where you will see the famous Priddy Hurdles stored under a thatch. They were used for the annual sheep fair, which still takes place in August. However, today, new hurdles are brought in for the occasion to avoid having to dismantle the stack.

● Panoramic views ● Iron Age hillfort ● Norman castle ● Coleridge's cottage (NT)

The hills above Nether Stowey

START Nether Stowey
DISTANCE 4¾ miles (7.6km)
APPROXIMATE TIME 2½ hours
PARKING Car park by library and Quantocks AONB Office
ROUTE FEATURES Moderate climbs, woodland and field paths may be muddy, quiet lanes without footpaths

This delightful walk begins in the picturesque village of Nether Stowey, where the poet Samuel Taylor Coleridge spent the closing years of the 18th century (Coleridge Cottage, 35 Lime Street. Tel. 01278 732662). It climbs on to the wooded fringes of the Quantocks and visits two 'castles' built in different ages, both occupying commanding hilltops that offer outstanding views surrounding countryscape.

Walk up Castle Street and keep ahead at a junction, signed Over Stowey. Ignore side streets, but bear left at a fork to pass below the castle mound, which then rises on your right. You will see it again at the end of the walk.

Beyond the crest, the lane shortly drops to a T-junction, where you should go left **Ⓐ**.

Although trees now cover most of **Dowsborough**, it was a bare hill when Iron Age defences where thrown up around its summit. The arboreal cover now obscures the surrounding embankments, but the view north is spectacular evidence of the commanding position it held.

After roughly 150 yds (137m) turn off on to a bridleway that climbs to the right. Shortly, after following a stream, a stile on the right takes the path that runs above the watercourse. Rejoining the stream higher up, the way emerges on to a lane beside a cottage **Ⓑ**. Turn left, cross the stream and then climb the hillside beyond. Just after a barn and cottage, take a track on

PUBLIC TRANSPORT Bus service from Bridgwater
REFRESHMENTS Pubs and tearoom in Nether Stowey
PUBLIC TOILETS Adjacent to car park
ORDNANCE SURVEY MAPS Explorer 140 (Quantock Hills & Bridgwater) and Landranger 181 (Minehead & Brendon Hills)

The hills above Nether Stowey WALK 13 **47**

the right that rises across open fields.

Higher up, where it bends left between white posts, bear right through a gate into a field. Continue with the fence on the left to another gate, just beyond the crest. Through that, walk ahead to the top-right corner, where a stile leads into a wood.

> **?** *What is the most common woodland tree on Dowsborough Hill?*

C Follow the track in front beside an ancient, outgrown beech hedge for about 150 yds (137m) to a crossing. There, turn right; the path then undulates and twists through oak and beech wood interspersed by more open areas of bracken and shrub-clad heathland. After some ¾ mile (1.2 km) the path ends at a lane.

> **Stowey Castle** was built by the Normans in the 11th century, a simple motte and bailey, that is, a central keep on a mound surrounded by an enclosed court. Although it was demolished some 400 years later, and the stone taken away for use in the construction of nearby Stowey Court, the earthwork and embankments remain a prominent feature.

D Cross to a gap in the low wall opposite and bear left on a rising path through the woodland above the road. When you reach a lateral track, turn right to climb Dowsborough Hill. Go forward at a junction, the ascent becoming more determined, and then take the left fork higher up. At a crossing track further on, go left, the climb now easing as you reach the crest of the hill. The way crosses a low embankment and continues ahead, shortly breaking into a small clearing.

E Return along the track by which you reached the fort, but continue past the junction where you turned up. Shortly beyond there, turn left on a waymarked track that drops down the side of the hill to a junction. There, go right through some of the oldest trees in the wood,

ultimately emerging on to a lane. Follow it left to a sharp bend at Walford's Gibbet, named after a forest charcoal-burner, John Walford, whose body was strung up there for a year after he was hanged for the murder of his wife.

Sheep wandering through the woods

F Leave the lane at this point, going ahead through a gate to walk down an open field. Bear slightly left to follow a descending boundary further on and continue losing height across the subsequent field. At the bottom, leave through a gate. Turn left along a hedged track, out to Hack Lane. Follow it right for about ¼ mile (400m).

Just beyond the crest of the hill **G**, cross a waymarked stile through the hedge on the left. Walk downfield, initially beside the left-hand hedge and continuing beyond its end; ahead is Stowey Castle. Over a stile at the bottom, turn left along a lane but then immediately walk right on to a track below the castle. A few yards along, go right over the second of two adjacent stiles and climb to the earthwork surrounding the central mound. The final ascent appears formidable, but an easy way up can be found on the far side. ●

14 *Around Fyne Court and Broomfield*

START	Fyne Court (National Trust)
DISTANCE	3½ miles (5.6km)
APPROXIMATE TIME	2 hours
PARKING	Fyne Court car park (charge)
ROUTE FEATURES	Woodland and field paths may be muddy after heavy rain, quiet lanes without footpaths

Beginning at Fyne Court, which houses the Quantocks Visitor Centre and the Somerset Wildlife Trust, this walk explores some of the rich woodland cloaking the deep river valleys that cleave the south-eastern corner of the Quantocks. There is much to look for amongst the trees, and the return along the top of the valley offers fine views across the hills to the south.

Return to the road outside the car park and walk left towards Broomfield church. Before you reach it, however, turn right over a waymarked stile into a paddock. Walk directly downhill to a double ranch stile and continue descending the subsequent field. Go right along the bottom boundary to find a stile leading on to a track by Rosegate Kennels.

Ⓐ Cross to another stile opposite and climb the open field beside its fence. At the crest of the hill, go through a gate on the right. Now bear left, crossing to a stile hidden in the far hedge to emerge on to a lane. Walk down some 50 yds (46m), passing a junction, and then go left, dropping quite steeply along a hedged track into Wort Wood. Over a stream at the

Only the library and music room survive from the 17th-century **Fyne Court**, that was all but destroyed by a fire in 1894. It was the home of the Crosse family, of whom the best-remembered member is Andrew. A philosopher and gentleman scientist, he was a pioneer in the study of electricity during the early 19th century. Local people christened him the 'Thunder and Lightning Man', because of the eerie flashes of light and explosive crashes that emanated from his workshops late into the night.

REFRESHMENTS Snacks and picnic area at Fyne Court
PUBLIC TOILETS Fyne Court Visitor Centre
ORDNANCE SURVEY MAPS Explorer 140 (Quantock Hills & Bridgwater) and Landrangers 181 (Minehead and Brendon Hills) and 182 (Weston-super-Mare)

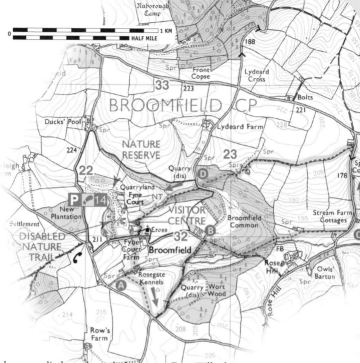

bottom, climb on through the trees to reach a junction of tracks at the corner of a lane.

Ⓑ Ignore the track immediately right; instead cross and then go right, along a path waymarked 'Quantock Greenway'. It falls back into the woods, shortly meeting the stream you crossed earlier. However, instead of fording it, turn left on to an initially indistinct path, following the course of the stream.

Eventually the way emerges over a stile into an open field. Strike out,

? *Who do you think carved the bench ends of the pews in Broomfield church?*

Young enthusiasts at Fyne Court Visitor Centre

crossing a bridge over a stream and walk on below an ornamental lake. Continue over another bridge to cross a stile, and there bear left uphill to follow the top border of the field. Keep the same heading through a couple of gates and on past a wooded garden to leave on to a lane. Take care, for the path drops directly on to the carriageway.

C To the left, the lane climbs steeply away, eventually reaching some cottages near the top. Turn left on to a track immediately before them and follow it across the fields above the valley. Further along, the way twists through a hedge, continuing on its opposite side. Gently descending and shortly narrowing to a path, it eventually emerges into the corner of a field. Keep ahead alongside an overgrown hedge to a stile beyond a massive old beech tree.

Back in woodland, follow a winding and occasionally indistinct path through the trees, dropping to cross a stream. Above the opposite bank, a more evident path leads left, soon losing height to a lane.

D Cross to a gate opposite, from which a track rises beside a wood along a shallow, open valley. Keep going to the top of the fields and continue climbing on a wooded track that ends at a stile into a field. Walk across the field and then leave through a gate on the right to reach a lane beside the church. Turn right and walk back to the starting point of the walk at Fyne Court car park. ●

A green lane follows the hills above Broomfield

The Parrett between Langport and Muchelney Abbey

START River Parrett Visitor Centre, Langport
DISTANCE 4 miles (6.4km)
APPROXIMATE TIME 2 hours
PARKING Car park at Visitor Centre
ROUTE FEATURES Riverside paths can be muddy and even impassable after prolonged rain, quiet lanes without footpaths

15

Not far from Langport lies Muchelney, a low island amidst the marshes. It was settled by monks in the 8th century, but the ruins are of a later abbey, founded around 950. This easy, level walk begins from Langport.

Eventually, a footbridge will link the Visitor Centre with the footpath on the Parrett's opposite bank. However, until it is built, cross by the road bridge and double back beside a tyre-fitting shop, where a gate leads to the riverbank. Follow a path beside the water for a little over ½ mile (800m) to its confluence with the Yeo at Huish Bridge.

The abbot's lodgings and ruins of the abbey church

? *What is the symbol marking the Parrett Trail on the way to Muchelney Abbey?*

PUBLIC TRANSPORT Bus service from Bridgwater
REFRESHMENTS Pubs in Langport, tearoom at Muchelney, picnic area by Visitor Centre
PUBLIC TOILETS Adjacent to visitor centre
ORDNANCE SURVEY MAPS Explorer 129 (Yeovil & Sherborne) and Landranger 193 (Taunton & Lyme Regis)

Following its destruction by Danish raiders, **Muchelney Abbey** (tel. 01458 250664) was refounded in the 10th century and survived until the Dissolution. The abbot's lodgings continued in use for another 400 years as a secular residence. Despite its isolation, Muchelney Abbey became wealthy. The 14th-century Bishop of Wells was not impressed with the monks' lavish ways and commanded a return to the austerities and disciplines of their Benedictine foundation. He also ordered the rebuilding of the adjacent parish church and the provision of a residence for its priest.

A Cross over and resume your progress upstream, the path signed to Muchelney. Keep going at the edge of successive fields until, eventually, you emerge at Westover Bridge **B**. Turn left and follow a lane into Muchelney. You pass behind the abbey ruins as you approach the village, but keep going to a junction by the village green. As you bend right in front of the church, the Priest's House then lies on your left. To reach the entrance to the abbey, continue along the lane.

C Leave the village by the same lane you came in on, but continue along it past Westover Bridge **B**, the way lined by pollarded willows. Beyond the buttresses of a dismantled bridge **D**, double back to the right

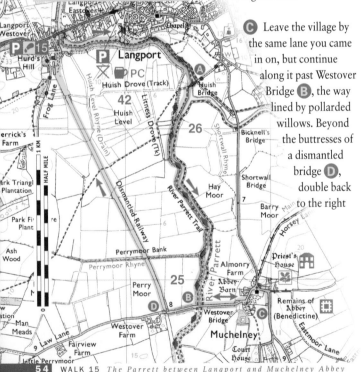

The **Priest's House** (tel. 01458 252621) is an attractive building with stone mullioned windows and a gothic doorway, and stands at the heart of the hamlet behind a wonderful country garden.

and pass through a couple of gates on to the course of an abandoned railway, signed as the Langport and Parrett Cycleway. The railway was one of those that fell under Dr Beeching's axe after his controversial report in 1963. The main line still runs through Langport to the north, but its station too has been closed.

Follow its raised course across the flood meadows to Langport.

Through a gate at the end, turn right and then left to bypass a small business area. Continue ahead along a road back to the visitor centre.

Enter Muchelney's church and you are immediately struck by its **painted roof**, executed in the 1600s and depicting angels, looking more worldly than heavenly dressed in Tudor high fashion. The floor tiles below the altar were rescued from the abbey's lady chapel – look for elephants and knights on horseback. The 19th-century organ is also a rare survival. By command of the bishop, the abbot had to maintain the parish priest with a daily allowance of bread and 2 gal. (9 l.) of ale as well as fish or eggs, with meat being substituted on Sundays and Tuesdays.

The 14th-century Priest's House

16 *Ham Hill and Montacute*

START Ham Hill Country Park

DISTANCE 4½ miles (7.2km)

APPROXIMATE TIME 2½ hours

PARKING Norton car park

ROUTE FEATURES Woodland and field paths may be muddy, moderate climbs

From the number of houses, halls and churches built of Ham stone, it is surprising there is any hill left, but at some 450ft (137m) high, it remains a fine vantage. To the east, beyond St Michael's Hill lies Montacute, an attractive village with a fine Elizabethan house. It was used as a location for the film Sense and Sensibility.

Stone Age tribes visited **Ham Hill** long before Iron Age people built a massive fort here, one of the largest in Europe. You can still see remains of its ditch and rampart defences. It was the Romans who began the quarrying of the beautiful honey-coloured limestone, an activity that continues today.

From the car park, cross to the grassy hillocks of old quarry workings opposite and bear left, taking a winding course to reach a toilet block and ranger station. From there, a track right rises to the Prince William Inn.

Early morning mist at Montacute

PUBLIC TRANSPORT Bus service from Yeovil to Montacute (alternative start)

REFRESHMENTS Pubs and tearooms in Montacute, pub and picnic area at Ham Hill

PUBLIC TOILETS Ham Hill Country Park and Montacute

ORDNANCE SURVEY MAPS Explorer 129 (Yeovil & Sherborne) and Landrangers 183 (Yeovil & Frome) and 194 (Dorchester & Weymouth)

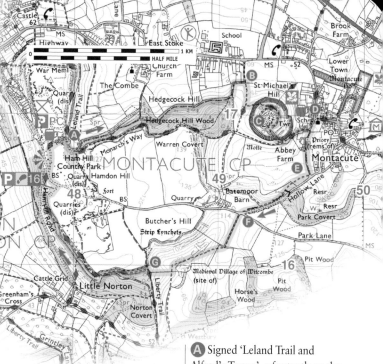

On the path to Montacute

A Signed 'Leland Trail and Alfred's Tower', a footpath on the right drops through a gate. Turn right to another gate into a wood and a junction of paths. Ignore a stile on the left, but then, a few yards on, bear left at the perimeter of the wood. Go either way where the path divides, but shortly descend steps on the left to continue on a lower path. Further on, past a ruined pump-house, the way undulates downwards,

> **?** *How many steps make the staircase up the tower on St Michael's Hill?*

Montacute House

eventually emerging from the wood. Continue left down a track and then go right at the entrance to a house. At the next bend, pass through a gate on the right into a field.

B Bear left, rising to a stile below the tree-clad St Michael's Hill. Climb ahead along a path through the wood, which later winds around to emerge to a clearing at the summit **C**.

> **St Michael's Hill** also has an Iron Age fort, the path up its steep slopes passing through the still impressive earthworks. The Normans built a castle too, which particularly angered local Saxons who believed a fragment of the Holy Cross had been found there. The tower now standing on the top was built as an observatory in 1760 by Sir Edward Phelips of Montacute House.

The direct descent is particularly steep so it is preferable to return to the point at which you entered the wood, where a path encircles the base of the hill. Follow it left to a stile. Over that, descend a grassy bank to a track and go left. The way shortly drops through a wooded cutting to a gate. Walk out past the old priory gatehouse and turn left to the church **D**.

Montacute House and the village centre lie to the right. Overlooking the village square, you will find the TV and Radio Museum, which, although small, is crammed full of fascinating memorabilia.

To continue the walk, return to the church and go left, but now continue ahead beyond the junction at the priory gatehouse, the way signed to Hollow Lane. Turn right at the top **E**, but after 10 yds (9m) enter a field through a gate on the right and continue above the lane along its edge. Eventually, at the top of the hill, you are forced back on to the lane.

F Cross the junction to a track, signed 'Witcombe' and walk on along the top edge of an open field. Where the track shortly turns left at a corner, bear right. A grassy trod drops across the valley, past the site of the abandoned medieval village of Witcombe at the bottom. The way then rises steeply to a wood above **G**.

Through a gate, turn right but

The 16th-century gatehouse, now part of Abbey Farm, is almost all that remains of Montacute's 11th-century Cluniac priory. Many of its stones were incorporated in **Montacute House** (tel. 01935 823289), built at the end of the 16th century for Sir Edward Phelips. It is remarkable, amongst other things, for its immense gallery, 189ft (58m) long. St Catherine's Church has some interesting Phelips' tombs. Have a look at the organ loft, supported on corbels carved with musicians playing an assortment of instruments.

then, almost immediately, go left on a track that undulates along the top of a wooded hillside. Ignore tracks off either side, but keep ahead, ultimately emerging into an area of grassy hillocks, the remnants of old quarry workings. Continue through, back to the car park. ●

Cottages in Montacute, built from Ham stone

17

Around Westwood and Farleigh Hungerford

START Avoncliff Aqueduct
DISTANCE 5½ miles (8.9km)
APPROXIMATE TIME 3 hours
PARKING Car park at Avoncliff
ROUTE FEATURES Moderate climb, field paths may be muddy, quiet lanes without pavements, canal towpaths

The Avoncliff Aqueduct, is the first of many features along this longer but straightforward walk. Canal boats, a 15th-century manor, ruined castle with an intriguing chapel and Italianate gardens all compete for attention.

The walk begins along the canal towpath on the opposite bank to the car park, reached via a track that passes beneath the aqueduct. Follow the waterway left towards Bradford-on-Avon for ¾ mile (1.2km) to a footbridge **Ⓐ**, cross and double back at the edge of a field. Carry on above the canal and then, over a stile, bear left up to a wood. However, ignore the gate there and walk left beside an overgrown hedge at the top of the

Originally a manor-house, **Farleigh Hungerford Castle** (tel. 01225 754026) was first fortified around 1370 by Sir Thomas Hungerford, the House of Commons' first Speaker. His son, Sir William, extended the defences some fifty years later to incorporate an outer court, and it is largely his work that survives today. Some impressive parts of the defences remain, and the chapel contains beautiful wall-paintings, fine stained glass and some amazing tombs of the Hungerford family.

? *Who is standing on the bridge overlooking the River Frome at Iford?*

PUBLIC TRANSPORT Bus service from Bath to Westwood (alternative start point), trains to Avoncliff
REFRESHMENTS Pubs and cafés at Avoncliff, Westwood and Iford Manor
ORDNANCE SURVEY MAPS Explorers 142 (Chippenham & Bradford-on-Avon) and 156 (Shepton Mallet & Mendip Hills East) and Landrangers 172 (Bristol & Bath) and 173 (Swindon & Devizes)

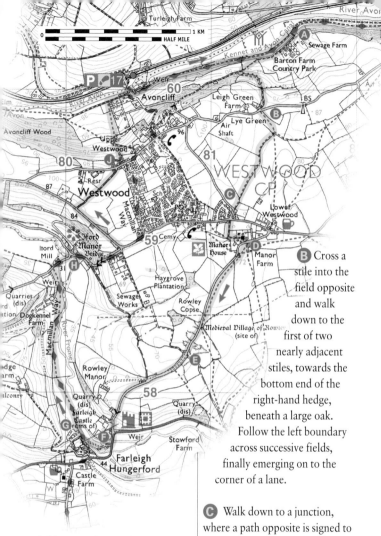

B Cross a stile into the field opposite and walk down to the first of two nearly adjacent stiles, towards the bottom end of the right-hand hedge, beneath a large oak. Follow the left boundary across successive fields, finally emerging on to the corner of a lane.

C Walk down to a junction, where a path opposite is signed to Westwood church. Follow it left at a bend and then past St Mary's Church on to a lane. The entrance to Westwood Manor (tel. 01225 863374) is then just to your left. Built in the 15th century and

field. Over a fence stile continue up, following an old hedge-line to a stile above. Keep going over a couple more stiles, shortly joining a hedged path to a cottage garden and out beyond it to a lane.

having some fine Gothic and Jacobean features, it was bequeathed to the National Trust in 1960, together with a wonderful collection of 16th- and 17th-century furniture.

D Cross to a stile opposite and bear right down the field. Continue alongside its right-hand hedge beyond a cottage until you are eventually returned to the lane. Enter the next field over a stile, some 15 yds (14m) along on the left. Although little more than low banks and shallow hollows are to be seen today, these fields were the site of an ancient village, Rowley. The earliest mention of a settlement is from 1001 and,

The ruins of Farleigh Hungerford Castle

although the village had been abandoned by the middle of the 16th century, there was still a farm here in the latter part of the 19th century. Continue along the field edge, before emerging once again, lower down the lane.

E You must now follow the lane for the next ½ mile (800m) down to its junction with the main road. Go ahead over the River Frome, but then turn right past a group of cottages along a drive **F**. Beyond the cottages, it leads below the foot of Farleigh Hungerford Castle. The entrance lies at the top of a stepped path to the left, but return here to continue the walk.

G Carry on along the track beyond the castle. As you approach the entrance of a trout farm, bear right over a footbridge and a couple of stiles into the corner of a field. A faint path meanders through successive meadows, following the river's course down-stream. It eventually ends at a lane. Turn right, recrossing the Frome to a junction in front of Iford Manor. During the first part of the 20th century, the manor was the home of the renowned architect and landscape gardener Harold Peto. He created the wonderful Italianate gardens for which the

A barge crossing the Avoncliff aqueduct

house is now known. They are open during the summer months.

H Turn right and follow the lane around the manor and steeply up to a junction at the top of Iford Hill. Go left along the main road for ¼ mile (400m) to the crest of the hill, where a bridleway leads right, crossing the fields to emerge at Westwood.

J Walk down the street to the right for 150 yds (137m) then leave on the left, between cottages, to a field behind. Continue down its right-hand edge to a stile, from which a rough path drops steeply through trees to a track. Turn sharp left and then follow it right to go

over a stile back into a field at the bottom. Keep on to reach a stile near its right, bottom corner out to a track. The Avoncliff Aqueduct then lies only a short walk to the right.

●

The first practical proposals for a **canal** between the Kennet and Avon rivers, to link the ports of Bristol and London, were mooted in 1788. But it was not until 1810 that its 57 miles (91km) were finally completed.

Several major problems faced its engineer John Rennie, including this crossing of the Avon and Avoncliff. His solution was an **aqueduct**, 175 ft (53m) long, which also carried a tramway beside the canal, used to bring stone from the quarries near Westwood.

Wellow to Stony Littleton

.8

START Wellow
DISTANCE 5½ miles (8.9km)
TIME 3 hours
PARKING Car park in Wellow
ROUTE FEATURES Moderate climb, field paths and farm tracks may be muddy, remember to take a torch to explore the barrow

The walk's highlight is undoubtedly the fine Neolithic burial mound above Stony Littleton, which occupies a commanding hillside position overlooking Wellow Brook. However, other attractions are the fine views over the surrounding countryside and the wonderful assortment of wildflowers that grow in the hedgerows. Wellow's church, at the eastern end of the village, is also worth a visit.

From the car park, return to the main street and go right into the village. When you reach a junction near the Fox and Badger, turn left. About 150 yds (137m) up the hill, leave over a waymarked stile on the left beside the gateway to a house. Walk on through a gate and, maintaining a diagonal line up the hillside, climb across the fields until, eventually, you emerge over a final stile on to a track along the top of the hill.

A Follow the track to the left. There is a wonderful view across the valley. On the opposite hillside, you can see the prominent mound

Relaxing in Wellow

PUBLIC TRANSPORT Bus service from Midsomer Norton
REFRESHMENTS Pub in Wellow
ORDNANCE SURVEY MAPS Explorer 142 (Shepton Mallet & Mendip Hills East) and Landranger 172 (Bristol & Bath)

The entrance to Stoney Littleton Long Barrow

of Stoney Littleton Long Barrow, which is visited later in the walk.

During the early centuries of the first millennium, this part of England became 'Romanised'. The countryside was extensively farmed, with estates centred on substantial villas, the comfortable homes of the wealthy landowners. Although no obvious sign remains, one such villa was discovered on the hillside west of **Wellow**. The well-drained, southward-facing slopes that surrounded it could well have been exploited for the cultivation of vines, something that is still practised in parts of the county today.

Where the way forks, bear left and keep going for a further ½ mile (800m), gently losing height before reaching a junction of tracks **B**. Turn left and walk down to Bourne Farm, continuing ahead through the farmyard and out to a lane beyond, Wellow Road. To the right, it winds steeply downhill to Double Hill Farm at the bottom of the valley.

C Turn left into the farmyard there and go through a gate beside the barns into a field, seemingly designated a cemetery for defunct agricultural equipment. Follow the hedge on the left through successive fields. Cross straight over when you reach a hedged track, Brinscombe Lane, and keep

? *How many burial chambers lead off the passage in Stoney Littleton Long Barrow?*

Horse riders in Wellow village

walk past it to a stile. Continue up beside the hedge to another stile and turn left, signed 'Stoney Littleton Barrow'. Go right at the next stile and climb to the mound.

E A path across the field from near the mouth of the chamber leads back to a track along the top of the field by a hedge. Turn left and follow it, eventually descending

going along the subsequent fields beside a stream that flows at the base of the hedge. Eventually, the stream falls away below you through a rough paddock. Keep ahead to reach a crossing track at the bottom of the final field. Turn right and walk out to a lane.

D To the left, the lane drops over Wellow Brook, rising again to a track leading to Stoney Littleton Manor Farm. Keep going through the farmyard and leave by a gate into the field beyond. A little further on, bear left towards a footbridge but, instead of crossing,

Stoney Littleton Barrow is a burial chamber, built to receive the bodies of a number of, presumably, important individuals. It was constructed by people of a New Stone Age culture about 5,000 years ago, some 500 years before the Egyptians embarked upon the construction of their Great Pyramid at Giza.

There is a long tradition of Christianity at Wellow and there may even have been a Romano-Christian church here. **St Julian's Church** is presumed to date from around 1370, constructed by Sir Thomas of Farleigh Hungerford. Inside, the impressive wooden roof is carried on corbels, carved as angels, and a magnificent screen separates the nave from the chancel. The Hungerford Chapel contains funerary monuments and on the wall are beautiful 15th-century frescoes.

to a lane at its end. There, go left, dropping to a ford and bridge over Wellow Brook. Continue up to a crossroads in the village.

Leave the church and return to the crossroads. Walk ahead past the Fox and Badger back to the car park.

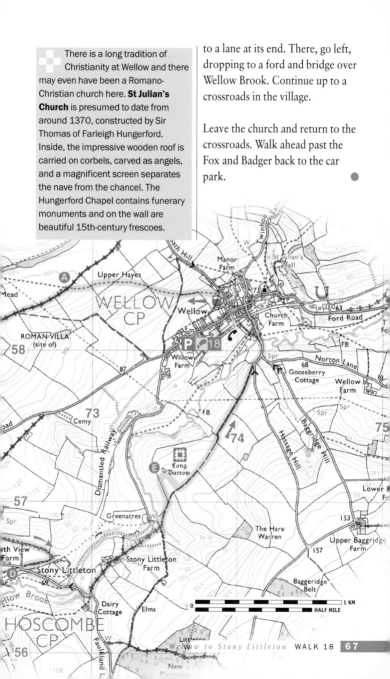

19 *Great Elm and Mells*

START Great Elm

DISTANCE 5¼ miles (8.4km)

TIME 3 hours

PARKING Roadside parking by river

ROUTE FEATURES River banks, woodland and field paths may be muddy, short section along busy road

Two deep, steep-sided valleys converge below the hamlet of Great Elm, each harbouring fast-flowing streams in the dense woodland foliage that cloaks their sides. This longer walk explores something of both, punctuated by a wander through the charming village of Mells. There is an ancient church in the village, and the way back passes overgrown ruins of a former ironworks.

From the road, just above the south bank of Mells River, a track leaves through a gate into the woods that line its upstream bank. However, instead of following the track ahead, immediately bear left through the gate, up a faint path into the trees. When you reach a track at the top, turn right and follow the edge of the wood for ½ mile (800m), eventually emerging on to a road.

Ⓐ Cross to a stile nearly opposite, from which a grass track leads around into a field. Continue beside its left-hand hedge to the corner. Ignore the stile ahead and,

The entrance to the village lock-up at Mells

PUBLIC TRANSPORT Bus service from Frome to Mells (alternative start)

REFRESHMENTS Talbot Inn at Mells at serves meals

ORDNANCE SURVEY MAPS Explorer 142 (Shepton Mallet & Mendip Hills East) and Landranger 183 (Yeovil & Frome)

Feeding ducks by the river at Great Elm

instead, go right along a tree-lined track. At the bottom, pass into a field on the left and walk on beside the right boundary, once again at the edge of woodland above Fordbury Water. Keep ahead along successive fields, until a final stile takes the way down a wooded bank on to the road.

B Take care along the busy road, which, to the right, drops into the valley and past the vehicle exit from the Whateley limestone quarry. Continue up the hill and, shortly after passing the quarry's upper entrance, leave at a waymarked stile on the left. A footpath follows the road below a steep, wooded embankment, which screens the quarry workings.

When you emerge from the trees, carry on along an open green swathe. Eventually, the path diverges from the road, following a line of overhead power cables towards an enclosed wood. However, before reaching the wood, veer off to remain beside the trees on your right. As you pass beneath more cables, turn right to descend through an opening in the trees. Emerging into a field below, walk across to a stile in its far-right corner and out on to a lane.

C Cross to another stile opposite and follow the right-hand hedge to a gap. Pass into the adjacent field and carry on beside the hedge and out to a lane beyond. Turn right and almost immediately bear off

Before the Dissolution, the manor of **Mells** was part of the Glastonbury Abbey estates. In the late 15th century, John Selwood, then abbot, embarked on a rebuilding plan to create a 'model village'. He got no further than New Street, the road beside the Talbot Inn leading to the church, before events overtook him. The estate was acquired by the Horner family, its former bailiffs under the abbot. However, there is no evidence that they employed the skulduggery implied by the nursery rhyme 'Little Jack Horner'.

right again, along a grass track falling through trees to another lane. Go right and then fork left to cross Mells Stream. Follow the lane up the opposite bank, bearing left at a fork to reach the main village street, opposite the entrance to the manor. Turn right and walk through the village.

D Beyond the Talbot Inn and New Street, bear right by the war memorial and walk down to the next junction. Ignore the first left turn beside the post office and, instead, fork left along a lane signed to Great Elm and Frome. After 300 yds (274m), leave along a bridleway on the right **E**, which winds into a narrowing and wooded gorge that contains Mells Stream.

You don't have to walk far before encountering crumbling

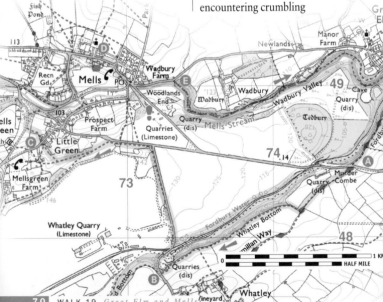

buildings. Now half-hidden by encroaching vegetation, they once housed an iron industry that filled this cramped valley. The main concentration of ruins lies a little further on, to the right where the path forks.

? *Who stands on top of the column above the war memorial in Mells and what is he doing?*

From the ruins, return to the fork and take the other branch. It rises behind the main buildings before returning to the riverbank lower down. Eventually, after passing a stepped path on the left, the track, now surfaced, runs below woodland gardens that drop behind houses, higher up on the valley side.

Leave the track at a waymark, bearing right across a grass clearing and carry on by the water to a footbridge. Cross and continue downstream on the opposite bank to meet a joining stream,

Fussells Iron Works was famous for the production of fine tools. Both the iron ore and limestone needed for its smelting were mined nearby and brought here, where the stream provided the power needed to drive furnace bellows and forging hammers. Be careful if you explore the ruins, for there are hidden holes where the river still gushes beneath.

Fordbury Water. Cross a bridge over that and turn left. A wide track then leads back to the road at Great Elm. ●

A shelter designed by Edwin Lutyens

20

Cheddar Gorge and Velvet Bottom

START Cheddar

DISTANCE 5½ miles (8.9 km)

APPROXIMATE TIME 3½ hours

PARKING Pay-and-display car parks in Cheddar

ROUTE FEATURES Steep climbs, woodland paths may be muddy and slippery after rain, unguarded cliff edges

The great chasm of Cheddar Gorge is one of the country's most dramatic and well-known natural formations, its spectacular caves drawing visitors across the world. However, few have discovered its continuation, Velvet Bottom. Beyond a disused quarry, lies a now-quiet and beautiful valley, once the scene of activity as it was mined for lead ore.

It is thought that **Cheddar Gorge** was formed during the ice ages. Torrents of summer melt-waters, unabsorbed by the permafrosted limestone, cascaded off the Mendip plateau exploiting a weakness to gouge out a canyon-like valley. The caves, on the other hand, were created by water gradually dissolving the stone, as it slowly percolated through cracks in the solid rock. In turn, the evaporation of the lime-rich water dripping through underground voids or trickling over rocks created the fantastic stalactites and stalagmites and other formations.

Follow the road from the village into the gorge. Past the millpond and almost opposite the tourist information centre, turn left on to a narrow lane. About 50 yds (46m) along, go over a stile up to the right, waymarked 'National Trust Gorge Walk'. Continue up over a second stile into a wood, where a path climbs steeply up a tree-packed gully. Eventually, the gradient eases and the path breaks into a clearing. Walk on through a gate at the top to a crossing track and turn right.

Ⓐ The route ignores side and crossing tracks, but two sensational viewpoints lie off the onward path.

PUBLIC TRANSPORT Bus service from Weston-super-Mare

REFRESHMENTS Pubs and cafés in Cheddar

PUBLIC TOILETS In Cheddar

ORDNANCE SURVEY MAPS Explorer 141 (Cheddar Gorge & Mendip Hills West) and Landranger 182 (Weston-super-Mare)

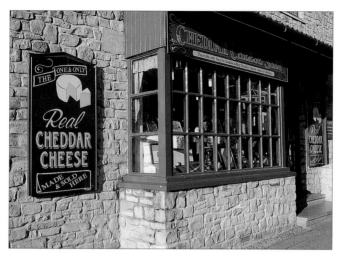

Real Cheddar Cheese on offer at Cheddar Gorge

The first is met a few yards on, to the right, over a wall. The second vantage is passed later, over a stile on the right. Further on, keep ahead over a stile, where the trees thin to give a panoramic vista across the gorge. Eventually, after another stile, the way begins to fall, steepening and finally descending steps to a wall-stile. Over that, a path crosses a grassy bank to a wood and over another stile. The way now winds down through the trees, finally dropping to a broad track at Black Rock.

B To the left, the track leads first past a lime kiln and then below a cliff, once quarried for its stone. A

> **?** *Pick up a piece of the black, glassy rubble from the slagheaps in Velvet Bottom and weigh it in your hand against a similar-sized ordinary stone. What do you notice?*

little further on, as the track leaves the National Trust Black Rock Reserve, go through a kissing-gate on the right into the Velvet Bottom Reserve.

C Walk ahead up the base of the valley, rising through the terraces of old ore settling pits. The way winds past a depression and old buddle pits (for washing the ore) and then bare, black mounds of

Lead was mined in **Velvet Bottom** before the Romans arrived, but the most intensive periods of working were during the Roman occupation and in medieval times. The mines were finally abandoned in the 1880s, and nature has since begun to reclaim the land. It is a slow process, for few plants can tolerate the still high lead levels in the soil of the valley floor. A leaflet, available at the entrance to the reserve, describes some of the plants and insects to look out for.

partial clearing just beyond, go right down a shallow gully and follow the wall around at the bottom to a gate, back at the foot

slag, the residue of the smelting process. Just past a wooden hut, which you will shortly see to the left, look for a stile across the wall on the right. Over that, climb the valley-side to reach an enclosed wood at the top, near Warren Farm.

D Turn right along the edge of the wood, over a stile below the farm and on to join a track dropping from it. Keep ahead, roughly parallel to a wall that lies to the left. The way gently loses height and, although the array of sheep and rabbit tracks may sometimes appear confusing, continue on the main path above the valley. After ½ mile (800m), look for a waymark fixed to a hawthorn bush on the left. In a

of Velvet Bottom. (If you miss the gully, the path soon peters out in bracken at the top of a rocky outcrop).

C Turn left and follow the drove back past the quarry and lime kiln, continuing through a gate and eventually on to the road at the head of Cheddar Gorge **E**. Cross to a path opposite, which climbs steeply through the trees on a right diagonal. Through a gate at the top, bear right at a fork and keep going over a stile, the way now

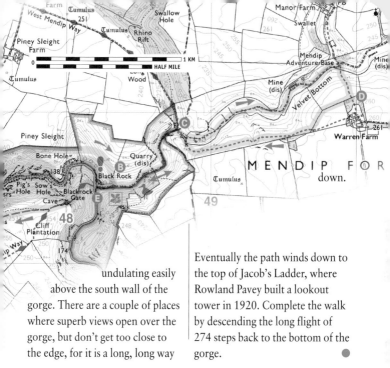

undulating easily above the south wall of the gorge. There are a couple of places where superb views open over the gorge, but don't get too close to the edge, for it is a long, long way

Eventually the path winds down to the top of Jacob's Ladder, where Rowland Pavey built a lookout tower in 1920. Complete the walk by descending the long flight of 274 steps back to the bottom of the gorge. ●

Black Rock used to be quarried for limestone

Further Information

Walking Safety

Although the reasonably gentle countryside that is the subject of this book offers no real dangers to walkers at any time of the year, it is still advisable to take sensible precautions and follow certain well-tried guidelines.

Always take with you both warm and waterproof clothing and sufficient food and drink. Wear suitable footwear, i.e. strong walking boots or shoes that give a good grip over stony ground, on slippery slopes and in muddy conditions. Try to obtain a local weather forecast and bear it in mind before you start. Do not be afraid to abandon your proposed route and return to your starting point in the event of a sudden and unexpected deterioration in the weather.

All the walks described in this book will be safe to do, given due care and respect, even during the winter. Indeed, a crisp, fine winter day often provides perfect walking conditions, with firm ground underfoot and a clarity unique to this time of the year.

The most difficult hazard likely to be encountered is mud, especially when walking along woodland and field paths, farm tracks and

Open fields below Walford's Gibbet

bridleways – the latter in particular can often get churned up by cyclists and horses. In summer, an additional difficulty may be narrow and overgrown paths, particularly along the edges of cultivated fields. Neither should constitute a major problem provided that the appropriate footwear is worn.

Follow the Country Code
- Enjoy the countryside and respect its life and work
- Guard against all risk of fire
- Take your litter home
- Fasten all gates
- Help to keep all water clean
- Keep your dogs under control
- Protect wildlife, plants and trees
- Keep to public paths across farmland
- Take special care on country roads
- Leave livestock, crops and machinery alone
- Make no unnecessary noise
- Use gates and stiles to cross fences, hedges and walls
          (The Countryside Agency)

Useful Organisations

Bath and North East Somerset Unitary Council
The Guildhall, High Street, Bath BA1 5AW.
Tel. 01225 477000

British Waterways
The Locks, Bath Road, Devizes, Wiltshire SN10 1HB.
Tel. 01380 722859

Council for the Protection of Rural England
Warwick House, 25 Buckingham Palace Road, London SW1W 0PP.
Tel. 020 7976 6433

Council for National Parks
246 Lavender Hill, London SW11 1LJ.
Tel. 020 7924 4077

Countryside Agency
John Dower House, Crescent Place, Cheltenham GL50 3RA.
Tel. 01242 521381

English Heritage
23 Savile Row, London W1X 1AB.
Tel. 0171 973 3250
www.english-heritage.org.uk
Regional office
Tel. 0845 3010 007

English Nature
Northminster House, Peterborough PE1 1UA.
Tel. 01733 455100
E-mail: enquiries@english-nature.org.uk; www.english-nature.org.uk

Ham Hill Country Park
Stoke sub Hamdon, TA14 6RW.
Tel. 01935 823617

Kennet and Avon Canal Trust
Canal Centre, Couch Lane,
Devizes, Wiltshire SN10 1EB.
Tel. 01380 721279

Langport & Parrett Visitor Centre
Tel. 01458 250350

Mendip Hills AONB
Charterhouse Centre, near
Blagdon, Bristol BS70 7XR.
Tel. 01461 463357; Fax 01461
463357; E-mail:
sj@somerset.gov.uk;
www.somerset.gov.uk/mendip

National Trust
Membership and general
enquiries:
PO Box 39, Bromley, Kent BR1
3XL.
Tel. 0181 315 1111; E-mail:
enquires@ntrust.org.uk;
www.nationaltrust.org.uk
Wessex Regional Office:
Eastleigh Court, Bishopstrow,
Warminster, Wiltshire BA12 9HW.
Tel. 01985 843600; Fax 01985
843624

Nine Springs Country Park
Tel. 01935 444558

North Somerset Unitary Council
Town Hall, Weston-super-Mare
BS23 1UJ
Tel. 01934 888888

Ordnance Survey
Romsey Road, Maybush,
Southampton SO16 4GU.
Tel. 08456 05 05 05 (Lo-call)

Public Transport
Traveline: 0870 608 2608

Quantocks AONB
Information Centre, Castle
Street, Nether Stowey,
Bridgwater TA5 1LN.
Tel/Fax 01278 733642;
E-mail:
quantockhills@atlas.co.uk;
www.quantockhills.com

Ramblers' Association
2nd Floor, Camelford House,
87-90 Albert Embankment,
London SE1 7TW.
Tel. 020 7339 8500

Somerset County Council
County Hall, Taunton TA1
4DY.
Tel. 01826 655455
Somerset Wildlife Trust
Fyne Court, Broomfield, near
Bridgwater TA5 2EQ.
Tel. 01823 451587